# NIGHTFALL

CURRENCY PRESS
SYDNEY

Joanna Murray-Smith

First published in 1999
by Currency Press Pty Ltd,
PO Box 2287, Strawberry Hills, NSW, 2012, Australia
enquiries@currency.com.au
www.currency.com.au
in association with Playbox Theatre Centre, Melbourne.

This revised edition published in 2011.
Reprinted 2011, 2012, 2016.



NATIONAL LIBRARY OF AUSTRALIA CIP DATA:

| | |
|---|---|
| Author: | Murray-Smith, Joanna. |
| Title: | Nightfall / Joanna Murray-Smith. |
| Edition: | 2nd ed. |
| ISBN: | 9780868199191 (pbk.) |
| Subjects: | Drama. |
| Dewey Number: | A822.3 |

Printed by Fineline Print + Copy Services, St Peters.

Typeset by Currency Press.

Cover design by Emma Vine, Currency Press

# Contents

For Sarah Jane Leigh
And as always, for Raymond

## PLAYWRIGHT'S NOTE

My thanks go to: Aubrey Mellor, Jenny Kemp, Jill Smith, Matt Cameron, Peter Manning, Ulu Grosbard, Kate Cherry, Helen Morse, Ian Scott, Margaret Mills, Margaret Cameron, Victoria Longley, Tom Healey, Tania Leong and all at Playbox; also to Katharine Brisbane and Currency.

Thanks also to Nita Murray-Smith and to Liz Mullinar and the many others who allowed me to share their memories.

Particular thanks to Raymond Gill for creative wisdom, and love more resilient than I deserve.

*Joanna Murray-Smith*
*October 1999*

*Nightfall* was first produced by Playbox Theatre Centre, Melbourne, at The C.U.B. Malthouse on 16 November 1999, with the following cast:

| | |
|---|---|
| EMILY | Margaret Cameron |
| EDWARD | Ian Scott |
| KATE | Victoria Longley |

Director, Jenny Kemp
Designer, Dale Ferguson
Lighting Designer, Rachel Burke
Composer, Elizabeth Drake

## CHARACTERS

EMILY KINGSLEY, a beautiful woman in her 50s
EDWARD KINGSLEY, an attractive, dignified-looking man in his 50s
KATE SASKELL, a woman between 35 and 45

*The setting for the play should exaggerate the strangeness of the proceedings by virtue of its naturalism. The sitting room and front foyer of a large English-style suburban house. The house is decorated in a tasteful, restrained English style: lamps, chintzy sofas, landscape paintings, books. The front door has a window beside it, but the large windows look out into the back garden. The house has an air of shabby grandeur.* EMILY KINGSLEY *is a still beautiful woman. She has a fragile weariness to her—her spirit has been crushed by her sensitivity to life.* EDWARD *is determined to survive life for both of them. She depends upon him. He depends upon her depending on him.*

*As the play opens, there is an air of expectancy and excitement to* EDWARD *and* EMILY. *They are playing a familiar game.*

EMILY: Door. Child. Nightfall.

EDWARD: Door. Child. Nightfall.

EMILY: Exactly!

EDWARD: A child comes to the door. It's nightfall.

EMILY: Yes!

EDWARD: A child comes to the door. It's nightfall. Inside... Inside a man and a woman wait.

EMILY: Yes!

EDWARD: It's nightfall. The doorbell rings. They open the door. On the porch stands a young woman.

EMILY: Yes! Yes!

EDWARD: They usher her inside. She is—she is—so—so extraordinarily—They can't quite believe—Her hair is the colour of—No. No. Too dangerous. A door. A child. Nightfall. That's as much as one can—

EMILY: I wish you could—I wish you could finish the story. But you can't. Not yet. Not yet.

EDWARD: It's five forty-five. It's five forty-five. Not long now. Another?

EMILY: Yes—

*He pours them both a new drink, handing one to her as the dialogue continues.*

EDWARD: A scotch. Two parents. A clock.

EMILY: A mother and a father drink a scotch while they watch a clock.

EDWARD: Yes—

EMILY: A mother and a father wait for—A mother and a father watch a clock, believing that at six o'clock—it might—things might—

EDWARD: You forgot the scotch. [*Beat.*] Yes. Yes. It might be—it could be over—

EMILY: Is it ever over?

EDWARD: It might be over—

EMILY: If things are—If—There's a lot to be—Who knows?

EDWARD: To pick up the phone. [*Beat.*] To hear her voice. [*Beat.*] It's looking up!

EMILY: [*delighted*] It's looking up! I feel—suddenly I feel—I'm scared to say it—as if I'm—

EDWARD: Moving—

EMILY: Yes! Yes! I'm so used to walking an inch at a time, a tiny step and after that another one, never looking further than an inch ahead. And suddenly I feel like running!

EDWARD: Yes!

EMILY: I feel like finding a beach, a deserted beach, and just running in bare feet—No! No! Running *naked*!

EDWARD *laughs.*

And howling like a banshee, nipples erect!

EDWARD: Let's do it!

EMILY: Can you imagine? Betty and Al Baillieau out walking Fromage and running to the book club, the new Isabel Allende in hand, with the news that they saw Emily and Ed Kingsley at the beach running completely naked!

*They laugh.*

And everyone will say: It's Emily! She's sick again! She's flipped!

EDWARD: Maybe we'll start something. A call to arms. The downing of whipper-snippers along the cul de sacs.

EMILY: The revolt of the aging suburbanites—

EDWARD: Or the Age of the revolting suburbanites—

EMILY *pulls herself back from her laughter.*

EMILY: [*thoughtfully*] Imagine if we all—if all of us—if we told each other the truth—

EDWARD: The truth about—

EMILY: If we told the McIntyres that we thought them nice people, but not very bright—If we told Rod and Meg that sometimes—in the middle of their slide nights on Vietnam—we just feel—desolate.

EDWARD: Well, no. No. We don't tell them and they don't tell us. And thank God for that.

EMILY: But don't you sometimes think it would be interesting—just *interesting*—to know what it is they—inside their houses—what they—

EDWARD: No.

EMILY: And perhaps somehow—if we said things—not cruel things—but somehow—*immediate*—If we said these things, we might not feel so—so—exhausted.

EDWARD: We agree—at a certain point, to oblige a contract—

EMILY: A contract of—

EDWARD: *Yes*. Of allowing others the same degree of delusion as one might wish for oneself.

EMILY: [*thoughtfully*] I did not. No. I made no such agreement.

EDWARD: It's getting—

EMILY: [*resigned that he will not meet her*] The light is fading—

EDWARD: Darkness is falling—

EMILY: It's five fifty—Can you? Did you? You left the gates open?

EDWARD: I left them—

EMILY: Are you sure?

EDWARD: Yes—It's almost dark. It's almost—

EMILY: Can you hear something?

EDWARD: Can I—?

EMILY: I thought I heard—tyres on gravel—

EDWARD: No. No, Emily.

EMILY: Tyres on gravel.

EDWARD: [*firmly*] No. [*Beat.*] You know, I had a dream last night that I had been living in a world without sound—

EMILY: Without—

EDWARD: The world had gone silent: cars driving through gravel, wind through birches, doorbells, party-goers: not a whisper. I lay in a state of—it was most peculiar—I lay without feeling. In a kind of vacuum. I wondered, for a moment if this was death—to be somehow conscious but without feeling. And then suddenly, the noise started. Earth music.

EMILY: The sound of tyres on gravel. If ordinary noises—cars tooting, trees blowing, builders building—if ordinary noises sounded like Mozart, do you suppose we'd play records of tooting and banging and blowing? Do you suppose we'd seek out 'earth music'?

EDWARD: Tyres on gravel? I think so.

EMILY: [*gravely*] *Make me happy.* [*Beat. Lightly, brightly*] Tell me again about the call—

EDWARD: I've told you—

EMILY: Just tell me again—To fill in time—To make me happy—

EDWARD: I said—

EMILY: No. No. Set the scene. You were—

EDWARD: You know all that—

EMILY: Just start from the—Pretend you never—A sofa. A phone call. A daughter.

EDWARD: I was reading on the sofa. You were in the garden with thingo—what's his—looking at the limes. It was lunchtime. The phone went. I lifted the receiver and said: Kingsleys. She said: Hello.

EMILY: Just—no—Just hello?

EDWARD: Yes. She was waiting for me to—But for a second I couldn't place—

EMILY: You couldn't place her—?!

EDWARD: You spend years coveting something, coveting something and then when you get it, sometimes you cannot recognise it. You're so used to the imagining. [*Beat.*] I heard her voice and I thought: I know it but—

EMILY: Not to know your daughter's—

EDWARD: I said: Cora. She said: Hello, Dad. I said: Cora—again, I think. I needed to be sure, although of course in saying 'Dad', well, it was obvious. I said: Where are you? She said: In the city. I don't think I said anything then. And she said: I'd like to see you. I think I just said: Yes. She said: If it's all right, perhaps Sunday late afternoon. I said: I'll come and get you. She said: No. I'll come to you. I think I said: Where? Where? And she said—very quickly: No. No. Let's not. Let's talk on Sunday. Before dark.

EMILY: Before dark—

EDWARD: That's right. So I said: Sixish then? And she said: Yes.

EMILY: And then—

EDWARD: The phone went dead. She said: Before dark—

EMILY: Before dark—

EDWARD: That's right. So I said: Sixish then? And she said: Yes.

EMILY: And then—?

EDWARD: The phone went dead.

*Pause as they take it in.*

EMILY: [*nervously*] She *will* come?

EDWARD: We have to presume—

EMILY: [*with the shadow of terror*] She will come?

EDWARD: Why would she—That's what I keep asking myself—why would she—make the call?

EMILY: That's right—that's right—

EDWARD: All those nights, we lay—

EMILY: [*quietly*] Don't—

EDWARD: Just to—just to see her. Remember how we'd sit in the windows of cafes—And say: Just a glimpse would somehow. Somehow we'd make do. We'd—just a glimpse. And we talked about how the physical has somehow been denied in modern—All the emphasis on the spiritual and yet to *see* something in an actual physical form. To see the flesh. One never quite gets over it. We sat in cafe windows. We always sat in windows. For years we've been explaining to maitre d's—

EMILY: The importance of a window. [*Beat.*] Tell me something. Who were we *before*—?

EDWARD: Before?

EMILY: Yes. Who were we—?

EDWARD: All parents have moments when they ask themselves what they once were.

EMILY: Don't they just grow into their new selves? Don't they just accept destiny without looking over their shoulders?

EDWARD: We all have moments—they just occur—wherever—at the ATM, tying up the papers on rubbish day, buying capers at the delicatessen—when it suddenly occurs to you that you existed in a prior universe. The universe of the childless.

EMILY: What did we do?

EDWARD: What did we do?

EMILY: In the universe of the childless.

EDWARD: God knows! [*Beat.*] Anyone without children has no excuse not to have written a novel.

EMILY: We were amused by each other.

EDWARD: Goodness.

EMILY: We thought the *Times* book review of the latest Norman Mailer was something to get excited about.

EDWARD: We read them aloud! [*Beat.*] She changed everything.

EMILY: Remember that time—in Paris—the first time, before Cora was born. I was staying in that little hotel where Oscar—was it? Oscar Wilde. And we had arranged to meet at that cafe. I got there first. And I'll never forget it—you coming around the corner, the shock of you. The beauty. The beauty of your being. Not to guess at you—

EDWARD: [*tenderly*] Emily—

EMILY: [*not quite to him*] There is such pleasure—pleasure and grief to see us then, see us—Oh look! There's Ed Kingsley. Young! And Emily Kingsley just coming around the corner of the Rue Bonaparte on their way to that little cafe for a Pernod. There they go. No idea at all about the 'course of true life'. The nervous problems she will encounter. The job upheaval he will face. The daughter they had—the one they clung to, the one they lost. [*Beat.*] A scotch. Two parents. A clock.

EDWARD: Sometimes her smell comes back—that musky smell—damp, shampooed hair—that musky warmth of a child in her pyjamas. The smell of newness. Which goes eventually, when we spend too long 'out there'.

EMILY: Remember the beginning?

EDWARD: [*gradually losing himself*] There she was. We called her Cora. Mad as hell, she was. For days and weeks and months and then—when was it, Emily?—around five months she actually started to *like* us. It seemed to me I had finally found myself some groove in the universe. All of it. Days of the week and tides and seasons and darkness falling and lifting… I suddenly knew how it was that great problems were solved, great poetry written—they were simply expressions of what it was to experience life as something compelling and intense. [*Beat.*] The only time in my whole life I felt that, was when I looked at that child.

EMILY: There was always a sense, wasn't there, that she was more than a little girl?

EDWARD: [*surprised by the depth of his feelings*] Yes.

EMILY: I mean it sounds odd, doesn't it—but she was somehow more—more than human. We sort of knew that was absurd, but that somehow it was true. You couldn't say 'otherworldly', you couldn't say how—but a sense that she—that she—

EDWARD: Knew things. Felt things. In a certain way. That made her different.

EMILY: For a long time I couldn't work it out—whether some children have an innate extra-ordinariness or if it is just that certain parents have an extraordinary faith. Faith or ego. That allows them to invest their children with imagined—greatness. I wondered. For a long time. But with Cora—I—I truly believe—She had a quality of—Well, perhaps that is simply 'beauty'.

EDWARD: Of course, one couldn't say one's child was—People would think you were mad—

EMILY: It's just not the thing you say—to other mothers at the kindergarten fund-raiser: Our child is Some Form of Supreme Being.

EDWARD: But you and I—

EMILY: Yes—

EDWARD: We knew—

EMILY: Perhaps that is, in the end, what kept us—what kept us—The conspiracy of knowing that.

EDWARD: Remember when I took her to school!

EMILY: You had to drop her off around the corner in case her friends saw the Mercedes! You had to hide like a—as if you had two heads—

EDWARD: She wouldn't let me take her to the school gates.

EMILY: She didn't want—No, you're right—She resisted feeling blessed. Why do fortunate children fear their good fortune? They worry that it makes them uninteresting. [*Beat.*] You opened the gate?

EDWARD: Jesus! Yes!

EMILY: You didn't have that tone—

EDWARD: That 'tone'—

EMILY: That slightly—that—The one that makes people afraid to—

EDWARD: What?

EMILY: That—

EDWARD: *What* 'tone'?

*Beat.*

EMILY: [*quietly*] That one.

*Beat.*

EDWARD: [*quietly*] Don't get hysterical. That's all I ask. Don't get hysterical.

EMILY: You're patronising me.

EDWARD: Don't—for God's sake—start all that! Just take a deep breath—

EMILY: No. You're right. It's not worth it. The gate is open, isn't it?

EDWARD: The gate is open. All right? The gate is open.

*Beat.*

EMILY: It's nearly dark.

EDWARD: We need to prepare.

EMILY: I bought the cheese biscuits from Patersons—the ones she loved. I made soup in case… depending on whether—how long—

EDWARD: I'm saying: We have to look 'not shocked'. We have to look all right. We don't want to make her feel—

EMILY: How does one—? I mean—how—?

EDWARD: Imagine the worst—that's the safest thing. Imagine she's cut her hair—

EMILY: Her beautiful—

EDWARD: The colour of—

EMILY: You mustn't say—

EDWARD: *We're* older, too.

EMILY: That's true.

EDWARD: *She* may be adjusting to *us*.

EMILY: We should have—I wanted the house to look—The carpet—

EDWARD: We're leaving—Whoever buys will just rip it—will just—they'll pull down walls, for God's sake.

EMILY: Imagine that. Ripping down the walls.

EDWARD: It's inevitable.

EMILY: What happens—do you think, to the energy—to the energy of what occurred within. Of the thoughts, the fights, the dreaming—the dreaming of a house—when the walls come down? What happens to the energy of a house?

EDWARD: The energy of a house? I've never thought about it. The walls come down. End of story.

EMILY: It was 'Bondage'—

EDWARD: It was—?

EMILY: The name of the carpet. Was 'Bondage'. It was neutral.

EDWARD: What are the carpets that *aren't* neutral called?

EMILY: She disliked privilege, but loved style. Isn't that the catch-22 of all intelligent, middle-class girls? Style, unfortunately, claims you virtually at birth. You can loathe good taste all you damn- well like, but you cannot disown it. Life is one long prostration before *the very expensive, simple things*.

EDWARD: It seems—suddenly—so long ago—

EMILY: Why do I remember her asleep so often? Was it that she never seemed safe there to me? I could not protect her in those journeys—

EDWARD: The sleeping journeys—

EMILY: Where she might fall from imagined trees, or be hit by imagined cars.

EDWARD: She whispered in her sleep.

EMILY: They sounded like words—As if she had these vital conversations in another place—a place we had no—these frantic whispers—

EDWARD: The language of dreaming.

EMILY: I'd get into bed at night and I'd feel this—all over me—a sense of dread—a sense of abstract doom.

EDWARD: She was too—Young children—It's too good—No one believes in that much happiness, so we have to invent—

EMILY: But was it a premonition? To be so suspicious of happiness? Some nights it was so intense, I couldn't speak. I was too captivated by it. I thought you'd say: What is it you're afraid of; and I knew I couldn't say. The end. The end was what I was afraid of. The end of—innocence. That's the only word I can—That somehow our life was dependent on an unspoken assumption that goodness prevails. That one's destiny has a moral compass. But that eventually something would happen. And from then on, we would become cynical. Cynicism. That to me was worse than death.

EDWARD: I would have understood—

EMILY: In this house we were too afraid to speak—to say—that one has no—

EDWARD: No—

EMILY: That one relinquishes—

EDWARD: That's right—

EMILY: And embraces absolute—

EDWARD: Yes.

*The doorbell rings. Neither one of them moves for a moment. They both stand.* EDWARD *moves across to the door.* EMILY *stands still, watching.* EDWARD *turns to her before opening the door.*

Whatever happens. I love you.

*This is an extraordinary statement for him. But he allows* EMILY *no time for response. He opens the door.* KATE SASKELL, *a well-dressed, well-groomed woman stands on the doorstep. There is a moment of silence.*

Can I help you? I'm sorry—

KATE *is very calm. She has an almost supernatural, sanguine quality, immensely assured.*

KATE: No, that's quite all—

EDWARD: You must want the McIntyres—They're the next one up—Spanish Mission—

KATE: The McIntyres—

EDWARD: With the dolphin.

KATE: The dolphin.

EDWARD: The topiary.

KATE: Oh! No. I want the Kingsleys.

EDWARD: [*surprised*] That's us. [*Beat.*] I'm so sorry. We were expecting—

KATE: That's perfectly—

EDWARD: Can I—?

KATE: You're Edward Kingsley.

EDWARD: Yes I am—

KATE: [*looking through to* EMILY, *hovering*] And you're Mrs Kingsley.
EMILY: Yes. Yes, but—Can we help you?
KATE: This is confusing—forgive me—
EDWARD: I'm sorry. We were expecting our—
KATE: I know.
EDWARD: We thought you were our daughter—
KATE: Yes—
EMILY: You weren't who we were expecting—
KATE: I'm here about your daughter—
EMILY: You're here about—You're here about Cora?—
KATE: That's right.
EMILY: [*panicked*] Has something—?
KATE: Goodness, no! No. She's fine.
EDWARD: We were expecting Cora—
KATE: I know that. Yes. I'm fully aware—You see, Cora sent me.

*Beat.*

EMILY: No—
KATE: Before you—don't panic because—
EMILY: She promised! She—
KATE: Hold on a minute. Just. Hold on a minute. First of all, she's fine. She's quite all right and yes, she's not far away. And she will come.
EDWARD: Oh. That's all. That's. All right then. So she is coming?
KATE: Could I—?
EMILY: She is coming then?
KATE: Look, if I could come in for a few moments and explain?
EMILY: [*ushering her in*] I'm very sorry. We should have—
KATE: That's all—
EMILY: Caught up in—
EDWARD: All the adrenaline—
KATE: It's natural—It's quite a day, isn't it?
EDWARD: We've been—You see today is the day—
KATE: I know—
EMILY: We haven't seen her, you see—not a word—
KATE: Seven years is a long time. [*Looking around*] What a very beautiful—an enchanting house.
EMILY: Thank you.
KATE: The aspect! The garden! Do you look after that yourselves?

EMILY: We rattle around it now. It's getting to be too much, to tell you the truth. We used to have—several—well, some years ago—we had a fellow—but now we try to—I'm afraid it's not—the rose beds are getting straggly.

KATE: The maples… there's a grandeur… You've been here—?

EDWARD *and* EMILY *consult each other silently.*

EDWARD: Oh, twenty—?

EMILY: Twenty-one—?

EDWARD: Around twenty—

EMILY: We were going to sell but it was our last link to [*beat*] Cora. [*Beat.*] Won't you sit down?

KATE *sits.*

EDWARD: We're having a scotch.

KATE: Thank you.

*He pours a drink and hands it to her.*

So. So. [*She smiles.*] A woman. Some parents. A daughter.

EMILY *and* EDWARD *look at her, shocked.*

Or should that be: A stranger. A sitting room. A question.

EMILY: You—you—?

KATE: Yes. Cora's game.

EDWARD: Cora told you about that?

KATE: Yes.

EMILY *and* EDWARD *look at one another.*

EMILY: She told you about that?

KATE: When she was a little girl. She'd write down three things on a piece of paper and you'd have to make up a story using those three elements.

EDWARD: That was her favourite—when she was small—She had an extraordinary imagination.

KATE: I imagine Cora was a very special little girl.

EMILY: She was. We always said: We were blessed. We'd come home from dinner parties and stand over her cot and just shake our heads in wonderment—-

EDWARD: In wonderment. We couldn't get over her.

EMILY: It felt as if there had to have been some mistake. We were just two ordinary people who happened to have this extraordinary child.

KATE: You never quite get over it, do you? The miracle—

EMILY: Exactly—

KATE: You just can't explain it, to people who haven't been through it—It's like some invisible, almost mystical connection for the rest of us—

EDWARD: Very true—

KATE: As if we have all been exposed to the same, radiant light of humanity.

EMILY: [*stunned, impressed*] That's beautiful. Isn't that beautiful, Ed?

EDWARD: [*non-committal*] Oh, yes—

EMILY: You have children then?

KATE: One girl. Yes. Keeps me busy!

EMILY: Oh yes!

KATE: Well, you know! You never stop worrying—

EDWARD: Quite. Quite.

KATE: You do your level best. But somehow that never seems enough. One loves them and one hopes—

EMILY: Exactly.

KATE: But one never knows. Quite who they are. We are caretakers only. One hopes they will be sound, spirited, loving. But life is not art-directed—

EDWARD: Indeed.

KATE: Cora has—I must say—Cora has a great capacity for love. For loving. She has a bounteous heart.

> EMILY *and* EDWARD *are disconcerted by this intimate assessment of their daughter.*

EMILY: [*nervously*] Well, that's—that's—lovely—

KATE: And courage. I want you to know that.

> *Beat.*

EDWARD: In our phone call last Tuesday, Cora did say that on Sunday—

KATE: Yes, at dusk—

EDWARD: Yes—

KATE: I understand that—Gracious! Where are my manners? My name is Kate Saskell.

EDWARD, *remembering his own manners, strides over and shakes hands.*

EDWARD: Edward Kingsley and my wife Emily. [*Beat.*] Scotch *before* the introductions! Very depraved!

KATE: Magnificent library—

EDWARD: We collect. In a modest way.

KATE: A very handsome edition of Gibbon.

EDWARD: Indeed. 1890. Emily used to be a bookbinder.

KATE: You used to—?

EMILY: Restoration work, mainly.

EDWARD: One of the best—

EMILY: Not really—

EDWARD: Did stuff for the British Museum at one point.

EMILY: I liked the feel. I liked the feel of the paper, of the vellum. I liked holding books in my hand.

KATE: That's so—Well, Cora—you know, has a 'sensitivity'—those expressive hands.

EMILY: She had beautiful hands. Long fingers like my mother.

KATE: But you no longer work—you said 'used to'—?

EMILY: I—became unwell for a little while. [*Beat.*] It slipped away from me.

EDWARD: My wife has always been a nervous person.

EMILY: It just slipped away from me.

KATE: I hate a room without books.

EDWARD: Exactly. So true—we often—

*He looks to* EMILY.

EMILY: Often! A room without books has no soul.

EDWARD: Say just that. What is a house without books? It's as if we're all so terrified of ideas these days, terrified by knowledge. You look at this emphasis on 'style'—

KATE: Style!

EDWARD: This reduction of things. Do we want a reduced world? Do we want to make good taste uniform?

KATE: I think many people find books just too threatening. Knowledge is frightening.

EDWARD: You're so right! The abandonment of history in our schools. History is too complicated. Let's all do the Mickey Mouse subjects—

KATE: The 'Mickey Mouse'—?

EMILY: That's what he calls them—'Business Studies', 'Communication' and so on—he's very naughty!

KATE: I see!

EDWARD: You open up the newspapers and it's all 'lifestyle'! Good God!

*As the conversation continues,* EDWARD *checks* EMILY*'s still full glass, takes* KATE*'s empty glass, pours himself and* KATE *another scotch.*

KATE: Espresso machines. French Provincial this and that.

EDWARD: [*for* KATE*'s benefit*] Meat grinding factories turned into 'New York-style' apartments. Of course a New York-style apartment is two foot by four foot and looks directly into an elevator shaft! How to use a Japanese dowry trunk as a coffee table. Perhaps they could slip a little world news in between telling us that the best way to serve a couscous salad is on a simple white plate.

KATE: A simple white plate!

EDWARD *hands* KATE *her refilled glass.*

EDWARD: A simple glass of scotch.

EDWARD *and* KATE *share the laugh.*

EMILY: Ms Saskell—excuse me, but did you happen to leave the gates open?

KATE: The gates—

EDWARD: [*to* KATE*, conspiratorially*] She's nervous. She's always nervous.

KATE: The gates are open. Yes. [*Beat.*] This must be all rather confusing—You've been very gracious—

EDWARD: Not at all. You're Cora's friend. [*Beat. Thinking, but without suspicion*] *Are* you Cora's friend?

KATE: Yes. Yes I am Cora's friend.

EDWARD: But she didn't come with you?

KATE: I came alone. But that's all—Don't panic. Because Cora, in all likelihood is going to come.

*Beat.*

EDWARD: 'In all likelihood'?

*Beat.*

KATE: Yes.

*Beat.*

EDWARD: Well, what does—?
KATE: Let's take this one step—
EDWARD: She said—
KATE: I know what she said—
EMILY: She said on Sunday—
KATE: Yes. Yes. I know. And there is every reason to believe she will come. Only you need—You see, she asked me—
EDWARD: Cora asked you—?
KATE: That's right—
EDWARD: Asked you to—?
KATE: To come ahead—to come—to speak with you—
EMILY: We're very—we know so little—We're—
KATE: I realise that—
EMILY: Her health, her—how she looks—
KATE: She's still thin. Yes. But physically strong. Her hair is cut—
EMILY: [*pained*] It's cut?
KATE: I don't want to—intrude upon her personal—That's very much Cora's right. To tell you in her own way. I'm just here to smooth the way. And I must say—I'm very pleased to be asked. By Cora. Because she's a terrific young woman despite everything—
EMILY: [*alarmed*] Despite—?
KATE: Whatever. And I'm not embarrassed to say I've been curious.
EDWARD: Curious?
KATE: I can see where Cora gets her strength from.
EDWARD: We try—
KATE: You don't give in—
EDWARD: [*proudly*] No. No we don't.
KATE: I can see that.
EDWARD: Thank you. I think it behoves one—to manage—
KATE: Even if it means—
EDWARD: Yes. A little pretence. Sometimes one rises to one's own charade and there's nothing wrong with that!
KATE: You've been through every parent's worst nightmare and you've held together.

EDWARD: One does one's best.

EMILY: I used to stare at parents in the street and wonder how it was that they got so lucky.

EDWARD: Now Emily—let's not feel compelled to 'share'—

KATE: No. I want to know.

EDWARD: That's kind—

KATE: No—Please—It's important that I understand.

EMILY: There's so few people to tell, you see. Edward feels that to speak—to speak of this is—

EDWARD: Only that for others, they don't want—even the kindest people simply don't want to be reminded that—

EMILY: Things happen.

KATE: Yes.

*Beat.*

EMILY: I used to listen to women in the green grocer on Saturday mornings, discussing the details of their children's twenty-first birthday parties. It used to be my—I used to close my eyes and see her, caught in photographs. The smart, champagne-coloured, silk satin suit I would wear with Ferragamo shoes. The party we would have… The nostalgic jokes that Ed would include in his speech. The trays of canapes. The ordinary string quartet playing Pachelbel's 'Canon' beneath the Japanese maple and Cora. Cora. Twenty-one years old.

EDWARD: People scoff at ritual. The repetition of things is deemed… tame. As if all our little rules and conventions are simply protection against… a brutal world. Well, perhaps they are. And so what? Shouldn't we comfort ourselves?

KATE: [*surprised, affected against her will*] That's—That's—Yes.

EDWARD: Cora considered happiness… insipid. She chose otherwise.

KATE: People walk away from their known worlds for all kinds of reasons. Fear. Yes, perhaps fear that they will be… enveloped. You hear about people leaving their clothes on beaches, pretending to have walked into the sea…

EMILY: Some don't pretend—

KATE: Yes. Fear. That's one reason. Boredom.

EDWARD: People lose their minds.

EMILY: We say they *lose* their minds, not that they ran away or that they vanished. We misplace them. As if we're too busy looking elsewhere.

KATE: And yet here you both are. Still together. Still upright. Still in the same house.

EMILY: We tried to give each other strength.

KATE: Of course! My God! You two have lived quite a life.

EDWARD: Well—We embraced opportunity.

KATE: Up until Cora was three years old you were in London, weren't you?

EDWARD: [*surprised*] That's right.

KATE: Then you got transferred home to oversee the company back here. That was Cora's school I passed—around the corner?

EMILY: Yes.

KATE: Miss Hatchett and the typing lessons.

EMILY: [*surprised*] She told you—?

KATE: Mr Fillipini who first explained to Cora that homosexuals were not people who had sex at home.

*They all laugh.*

EMILY: How do you—I mean, did Cora—?

KATE: Cora has told me absolutely everything, Mrs Kingsley—

EMILY: Emily!

KATE: Because friendship is about trust and if she trusts me I can help her. Trust is the single most beautiful word in the human language.

EMILY: [*disconcerted*] Oh—Oh—Yes—

KATE: Cora and I have no secrets. We spent a lot of time talking about her history, right here—where we're sitting—in this house.

EMILY: And what did she—I mean—we had—

EDWARD: A good—

KATE: She drew a picture for me. And Cora is so—eloquent—her words—

EMILY: Eloquent?

KATE: Edward—off to the city each morning in his chauffeur-driven Mercedes, enjoying the perks and responsibilities of a Managing Directorship. You helping out at the school, raising funds for the new performing arts wing—

EMILY: Oh well—the way you say that—it all seems very ordinary—

KATE: For most of those years Cora was doing well, seemed well-adjusted, if slightly rebellious, which is what you both expected and indeed, considered normal.

EDWARD: That's true. But how do you—?

KATE: And then one day—Let's see—when she was sixteen—

*Silence.*

EMILY: I made her breakfast. She said her coach had said she needed new tennis shoes. She complained that Edward wouldn't let her stay at the party on Saturday later than eleven even though the other girls—well—He was too… I asked her if she'd like rosemary chicken for dinner and she said yes. I kissed her. She smelt of wisteria—talcum powder—She—I'll never quite rid myself of—the way she threw her schoolbag over her shoulder—she had a way of—that cavalier toss of the bag onto those shoulders—something so compelling about girls that age, their boyish movements clashing with their growing womanliness—sort of, hopelessly rejecting it, yet proud, too. She smiled. I turned away. I was thinking that Jean Godfrey wanted to borrow my twelve-inch cake tin. And the door closed… And that was—yes. [*Pause.*] She never wrote or rang.

EDWARD: [*to* KATE, *conspiratorially*] Do we need to—? I mean, it's over.

EMILY: We went to the police and the missing persons people. Her face was in the Sunday Supplement. We had ads, rewards. Fifty thousand dollars for information. We talked to Cult People, even Interpol. She was listed on the National Missing Persons' Helpline. We had private detectives—We mortgaged—Well, that's why we have to—We put everything we had into finding her. There were sightings. Someone saw her on a train up north—someone saw her in a shopping mall. They even did DNA testings on—on—body parts found—And nothing. Then a year later, the police called us. They had information. They said: She isn't dead. But you have to accept, she doesn't want to be found. We begged them—we—but she had the right—

KATE: Yes.

EMILY: *She* had the right—not us—not us—It's not a right we discuss very often. But it's there for anyone who wishes to take it up. The right to vanish.

KATE: And on a certain level, it would probably be easier if she were dead—

EMILY: [*guiltily*] Well—

KATE: Simply to have closure. Closure is very important. As our experience of life deepens, it is not only daughters that we lose—but certainty.

EMILY: The night just brings—We find at nightfall—There is terror. We've both become sleepless—

KATE: Yes—

EMILY: And to some extent—We don't like to go out—

EDWARD: We used to be very—(sociable.) Parties!—Luncheons!—

EMILY: But it becomes too confusing—to discuss censorship and the movies—or—or—Balinese resorts and at the same time, feel this—this—

EDWARD: Terror.

EMILY: The police said: She isn't dead, but. You have to accept, she doesn't want to be found—

KATE: Yes—

EMILY: She doesn't want to be found.

*Silence.*

KATE: I want to make this as easy and as simple as I can. I'm here to help—

EMILY: [*not hearing*] She was our daughter. Cora Jane Kingsley. And then one day, she went away. And she never came back.

*Pause.*

KATE: Cora has—been through—a great deal. And she needs to rebuild her—her faith. Her righteousness.

EDWARD: Her righteousness?

KATE: It's important to Cora to be righteous. I am here to make that process safe for her—

EDWARD: But when will we—? I mean, she is—?

KATE: I fully expect so—

EDWARD: But what does that—I mean, what is it depending on—?

KATE: Well, it's depending on you.

EMILY: On *us*?

KATE: It is depending on whether Cora feels safe.

*Beat.*

EMILY & EDWARD: [*together*] Safe?

*Beat.*

KATE: That's right—

*Beat.*

EDWARD: We're her parents.

KATE: Yes.

EDWARD: She couldn't be safer than with us—

KATE: I can understand why you think that.

EMILY: I don't—I don't quite—

KATE: Let's not rush it—

EDWARD: But why wouldn't—? [*Beat. Dawning on him that he has no idea*] *Who are you?*

KATE: I'm a friend to Cora.

EDWARD: How do you know Cora?

KATE: She came to me.

EMILY: Where—I mean—where was this?

KATE: That's for Cora to—If she so chooses. The point is that when I first met Cora she was—I don't want to alarm you but—She was in a very bad way.

EDWARD *and* EMILY *sit in silence, very tense.*

Extremely thin. Very anxious and deeply—chronically—depressed. She'd been—travelling—She'd seen a lot—got mixed up in—Damaged.

EMILY: [*quietly distraught*] Damaged?

KATE: She needed a great deal of support and some practical help. Her state of mind was… precarious.

EDWARD: [*politely*] Well thank you. Thank you for helping her.

EMILY: [*tentatively*] And now?

KATE: She is getting stronger all the time. She finds beauty in the simplest things: music, flowers, cooking.

EMILY: Cora cooks?

KATE: She made me rosehip jam. She responds to the seasons. She is one of those people who is very much in tune with the universe—Notices the drift of clouds—

EMILY: Cora notices the clouds?

KATE: She despises the way human beings have come to ignore nature, as if it could be ignored. She is opinionated! Oh, indeed! But she needs to be handled very carefully, even now—

EMILY: My God—Oh, My God—

KATE: As I say, she's very much better.

EDWARD: So what can we—I mean, what do we need to do for Cora to agree to come home?

KATE: Well, that's a good question, Ed. What we need to do is go back over some—some details—When Cora was young—

EDWARD: What about when she was young—?

KATE: Just try to relax, Ed—

EDWARD: I'm not—

KATE: Look at that body language—

EDWARD *looks at himself. He drops his arms, relaxing himself in a self-conscious way.*

I'm here to help.

EMILY: Thank you.

EDWARD: I don't see why this is relevant. I don't understand.

KATE: Cora was your only child, wasn't she?

EMILY: We wanted more. But we had trouble—It didn't happen.

KATE: [*drawing him out*] She was indulged—

EDWARD: She wanted for nothing. Piano lessons! Ballet! Doll's houses! It's all—there—her room—it's all—Exactly as—

KATE: And emotionally—?

EMILY: We were a—*are* a—very close-knit—That's why this all—Suddenly she just—

KATE: A hostile act in a sense—

EDWARD: I don't know if Cora intended—I mean the way you put it—'A hostile act' has the suggestion of—I don't know that Cora intended to cause us—I mean, children are selfish—

KATE: Are they?

EDWARD: Well, yes. Yes. I mean that's what children are. They don't think. And as a teenage girl, it was my feeling she had—girls and their—well, you know—A competitive—

EMILY: With me, he means. He thinks it was my—

EDWARD: For God's sake—it's not an—

EMILY: That I—That Cora was—made vulnerable—

KATE: Made vulnerable—?

EMILY: That with my—my problems—

EDWARD: I never said that—Emily—I—

EMILY: That Cora inherited a—

KATE: That you—

EMILY: Yes. That Cora was inclined towards a kind of—

EDWARD: No!

EMILY: Weakness.

EDWARD: Girls and their mothers. That's all I—

EMILY: I tend towards… disorder.

EDWARD: [*sadly*] I never said that, Emily.

*They share a glance—it is the first time he realises that she knows what he has been thinking.*

KATE: And girls and their fathers?

EDWARD: It's different. It was less complicated. We were very close. We were very, very close. She was Daddy's little girl.

EMILY: In any case, she felt—I think she felt smothered—

EDWARD: As if the accoutrements of a middle-class life impeded her sense of—her sense of—who she was. That's our belief. That perhaps she was too—loved.

KATE: Too loved?

EDWARD: Felt compromised by—

EMILY: As if her life lacked—texture. She needed to feel—resistance.

EDWARD: So when she—when it—We assumed—

EMILY: The wrong people—

KATE: The wrong—?

EMILY: Yes—Yes—The wrong—

EDWARD: Crowd. She must have fallen into—

EMILY: It happens.

EDWARD: You see, we were so 'right'. So *right*. And she was attracted to—what we were not.

KATE: You're very clear about this.

EMILY: We've had a long time to think.

EDWARD: We were very close. Very tight-knit. Aren't we, Emily?

EMILY: [*lacklustre*] Very. Very tight-knit.

EDWARD: And Cora knew she came from a very happy, the happiest of unions.

KATE: 'The happiest of unions'.

EDWARD: You're thinking we 'protest too much'. That those who declare themselves to be happy, do so as a defence against their unhappiness. Isn't that what you're wondering, Ms Saskell? The truth is, we love each other. I'm not embarrassed to say it.

KATE: Why would you be?

EDWARD: Because we're not the kind of people who wallow in emotion.

KATE: No.

EDWARD: I don't believe in spilling your feelings. I don't agree that it's best. I don't agree that it's healthy.

KATE: Interesting.

EMILY: [*apologetically*] He loves playing devil's advocate! Edward's always had a healthy scepticism about what's fashionable.

KATE: Isn't the healthiest thing—

EDWARD: The healthiest thing is to *repress* your feelings. Do exactly what the experts tell you not to do. Stifle them. Pretend they'll go away. Because most of the time, our feelings *do* go away. Let's talk about *doing* things. Let's fill the void with the sounds of people who occasionally do more than feel something. Let's stop rewarding people for admitting: 'I feel angry', 'Fabulous!', 'Well done!', 'What a big step!'. [*Beat.*] *Fuck feelings.*

EMILY: Edward isn't so much a comedian as a stand-up belligerent.

KATE: I'm wondering if you feel the need to stress—the cheerful face of things—as a defence against blame.

EDWARD: Well—

KATE: Even strong families can—start to—can tremble—when things are in jeopardy.

EMILY: When the natural order of things starts to—shake.

KATE: Perhaps jeopardy *is* the natural order of things. I'm talking about when the domestic world begins to look as if it has been furnished—

EMILY: You're talking about dinner parties. You're talking about shopping for a new pepper grinder or contemplating an Easter brunch for twenty.

KATE: Yes. All right. Times when those rituals fall away from us.

EDWARD: We don't live in a perfect world—Scotch before the introductions, etcetera.

KATE: It's difficult when you believe you marshall the forces in your life to find that the forces marshall you. You had a golden run and then—

*Silence as* EDWARD *takes in her inference.*

EDWARD: We led a very good life, I don't mind saying—The golden days of the company culture—They rewarded loyalty—

EMILY: Holidaying all over the world, a country place—we never thought twice about expensive restaurants. Some of the parties!

EDWARD: We threw legendary parties. I mean, 'legendary'!

EMILY: The seventies and eighties. You can imagine. Lobster. Orchestras over the pool. Once we had a—

EMILY & EDWARD: [*together*] Bellini Party!

EMILY: It wasn't all conspicuous consumption. We sponsored a little girl in Uganda. She wrote us letters.

KATE: And then it ended.

EDWARD: The London office decided to restructure—

KATE: I've experienced similar things—believe me when I say, I understand.

EDWARD: That's very nice of you, Ms Saskell, but to tell you the truth I abhor the camaraderie of the aggrieved. And, in a sense, it freed me—I recognised what was important. Realised how insular that world is. Yes.

KATE: In a situation like that—even the strongest-willed people can experience—an erosion—

EMILY: He drank a little bit—

EDWARD: Hardly! For goodness sake, Emily!

EMILY: [*hurriedly*] It was never a problem, even then—

KATE: But you could feel yourself slipping—

EDWARD: [*capitulating to* EMILY*'s panic*] It was about respect—

KATE: And power. You'd been in a position of calling the shots.

EDWARD: I'm not embarrassed to say that's true, why should I be?

EMILY: It was worrying, but it wasn't calamitous. He got a very generous golden handshake.

KATE: But it was a shock, nonetheless. You'd effortlessly acclimatised to success… And suddenly, a brutal reminder that all the coveted trappings of a life are transitory. Within—deep within—we live another kind of life.

EDWARD: I needed no reminding—I'd worked too hard for too long. I had a family. And interests. Yes. Interests… My books…

KATE: It's all in the detail, isn't it? It's the look that passes between two young men as you walk past the water fountain. It's that moment when you stand in front of your desk with a cardboard box. It dawns on you as you hold a half-empty packet of H2B pencils and a luminous yellow post-it pad: You're worthless.

EDWARD: I never questioned my own worth!

KATE: You never had a moment of doubt?

*Silence as* EDWARD *takes in the truth.*

EMILY: It was no reflection on Ed—None at all—It was just—

KATE: I know—

EMILY: The world's gone mad—

KATE: Wasn't the day you were sacked the first time you realised the whole thing is a house of cards?

EDWARD: I wasn't sacked! I was retrenched. There's a difference!

KATE: Oh come now! You were *sacked.*

EDWARD: [*tension building*] Look—is this—? I mean—

KATE: [*ignoring his protestations*] Once you spent your days basking in the sheen of your waxed Mercedes, enjoying the fine, well-appointed systems of a company life. And then—smash! You're naked, staring at the clouds, contemplating death. And all of it vanishes: the chalet, the beach-house, the boat—they shimmer and shudder, they grow pale and distant, they hover on the horizon, and then they sink. Farewell to the parties, the legendary parties. 'And I mean, legendary'!

EMILY: He never went back to that level.

EDWARD: I started working for a very small firm. Ironically, I helped them restructure. We had to—adapt.

KATE: How long were you unemployed for?

EDWARD: Twenty-eight months—

KATE: And during that time—

EMILY *and* EDWARD *look at one another.*

EDWARD: We managed.

KATE: How do you think Cora reacted to all this?

EDWARD: We shielded her. And we were hardly on the street.

KATE: [*smiling, sympathetically*] Of course. It's not that you were ruined financially. It's more the erosion of the spirit. I've been through—Let me just say that my life has not been singularly enchanting! Believe me, it's not a phrase I use often, but as they say 'shit happens'.

EMILY: Quite! Yes! Goodness!

EDWARD: We've had our share of ups and downs, like any—

KATE: I'm not talking about ups and downs, Ed. I'm talking about catastrophes of the soul.

EDWARD: Now you've lost me. I'm not very Eastern. I'm sure Balinese orchestras are simply terrific, but I like my Mozart. I'm afraid I'm going out on a limb here, but I think the soul is a private thing and rather over-stated.

KATE: When my husband left me I prayed for death. At that time, I had no feelings left for others, even my daughter. I was consumed with the desire to disappear. I had lost faith in my aloneness.

EMILY: [*affected*] Oh…

KATE: We need to embrace catastrophe. Goodness, honour, fidelity—these things come from agitated souls, not complacent ones.

EMILY: Embrace it… That would be… I think I see…

KATE: Catastrophe is passionate. It floodlights the dark rooms within us—

EMILY: I think I—yes, yes!

EDWARD: The dark rooms? I'm sorry, but one gets on with things.

KATE: You can avoid them. You can walk around the dark rooms. But they are there.

EDWARD: No.

EMILY: Yes. Yes.

KATE: You understand—

EMILY: There are places we're too frightened to go—

KATE: Yes—

EMILY: Too terrified—

KATE: Yes—

EMILY: There have been times I've ventured there—

KATE: I know—

EMILY: And there was—even though I nearly—despite that, there was a relief—

KATE: I know—

EMILY: Not to skirt the darkness but to wade into it—

KATE: Some call it madness—

EMILY: To me—those 'dark rooms' had a kind of grace to them. I belonged in them.

KATE: As if—

EMILY: I was alive inside them. Whereas this—

KATE: Here—

EMILY: Was madness. Perhaps—It appears safe—it appears safe. But aren't we safest where we are most ourselves?

KATE: Yes.

EMILY: Marriage—well, we are what we compose ourselves to be in the light of each other. And whatever else we are stays in the shadows.

*Silence as the two women savour their communion.*

EDWARD: Oh fine. Oh, terrific. That's helpful.

KATE: [*to* EDWARD] Now there were times, perhaps, when you glimpsed your own—dark rooms.

EDWARD: No—

EMILY: [*irritated*] Oh, come on, Ed!

EDWARD: What is this? I mean, where are we? We are waiting for Cora. We are waiting for Cora.

EMILY: It's true, isn't it? Places we don't wish to go.

EDWARD: Yes. Yes. Places we don't wish to go. All right. But as you say, we don't wish to go there.

EMILY: Perhaps—

EDWARD: No. [*Beat.*] Listen, Ms Saskell—I'm sorry but—We're not clear on who you are exactly—

KATE: I think I explained that Cora asked me—

EDWARD: Yes, but *why?* We haven't seen our daughter in seven years. For years we've been in a state of—She told me she was coming today at six o'clock. And instead of Cora, you're here. And I'm sorry if this sounds rude, but I want to know why.

KATE: Cora needs to be certain of some things.

EDWARD: What things?

EMILY: What kind of things?

KATE: That it's not going to be ignored.

EDWARD: What? *What's* not going to be ignored?

KATE: All of it. All of it. The things that happened.

*Pause as* EMILY *and* EDWARD *take this in.*

EDWARD: *What* things?

KATE: It's very important to her, that you two should understand that under no circumstances will she agree to forget about it.

EDWARD: Forget about what?

KATE: What went on.

EDWARD: Where?

KATE: Here. In this house.

*Beat.*

Look, I'm not here to seek retribution.

EDWARD: [*stunned*] Retribution?

KATE: But I am looking for acknowledgment of what happened. Then Cora feels safe.

*Beat.*

EDWARD: *Who are you?*

*Beat.*

EMILY: Do we know what happened?

KATE: I think you do.

EMILY: [*panicked*] But I can't think! I can't think! What happened? I just can't think! Ed? Ed? What is it? What is it, Ed?

EDWARD: [*deeply suspicious*] You're not Cora's friend.

KATE: What do you—?

EDWARD: You're some kind of—What are you?

KATE: I serve nothing but my own moral authority. And I am an intermediary.

EDWARD: [*coldly*] What is this about?

KATE: It doesn't help if you—take that tone—

EDWARD: [*astonished*] I'll take any tone I like. This is my house. We don't even know—

KATE: You can deal with me or not, Ed. But if you don't listen to me, then you have no chance at all of seeing Cora.

*Beat.* EDWARD *swallows his scotch in a gulp. He carefully replaces the glass.*

EDWARD: [*with self-conscious calm, forcing himself*] Could we start again, perhaps? Could we—You see, Cora's mother and I are unsure about—

KATE: How do you know?

EDWARD: How do I—?

KATE: You say: 'Cora's mother and I'. How do you know you speak for Cora's mother?

EMILY: Well he does—I mean—

KATE: But how does *he* know that?

EDWARD: Look, excuse me, excuse me, but this is my wife and my house—and I don't think it's up to you—to you—to tell me how I might speak.

KATE: I'm interested. That's all. Because it's all related.

EDWARD: What's all related?

KATE: The way you speak for your wife. Or your daughter. I'm not criticising, I'm simply observing, that the language you're using is 'proprietorial'—

EDWARD: 'Proprietorial'?

KATE: 'My' wife, 'my' house. You are claiming the right to speak for your wife, but where does that right come from? Is it given or is it assumed?

EDWARD: Well that's—I mean that's absurd—

KATE: So you have a tendency to assume control?

EDWARD: We're not here to discuss me—

KATE: How do you know that?

*Beat.*

EDWARD: What is it that Cora wants?

*Beat.*

KATE: She wants an admission.

EMILY & EDWARD: [*together*] An admission?

KATE: Because once it's acknowledged, the healing can begin. And she's ready. That's the wonderful thing. And if she heals, then you can start to heal.

*Pause as* EDWARD *and* EMILY *take this in.*

EMILY: What did we do?

*Beat.*

KATE: I can promise you that what is happening here this evening remains within this house. Cora has given her assurance—

EMILY: Her assurance?

KATE: Unless you prove unwilling to co-operate, there is absolutely no threat whatsoever—

EDWARD: Unwilling to co-operate with *what*?

KATE: With the truth.

EDWARD: If we do not say whatever it is—whatever it is, this imaginary thing, if we do not say it then we will not see our child again?

KATE: That is the reality. Please don't attempt to intimidate me.

EDWARD: I can't—! This is—!

EMILY: Calm down, Ed. Just, calm down.

EDWARD: I'm not taking this—

KATE: [*standing*] I can leave.

EMILY: Please! No! Please don't leave!

KATE: Cora is being exceptionally generous. Many people in Cora's situation would not be prepared to address this so—so—informally. Now I realise you're both shocked, so I'm prepared to be understanding. But neither Cora nor I will be insulted. No. And if I am insulted then so is she. So listen carefully, I can leave, but when I go, I take with me Cora.

EDWARD: You're blackmailing—you're—! You're telling me—?

EMILY: [*panicked*] Calm down Ed. I beg of you! I beg of you! Please, Ms Saskell. Please don't go. We'll all calm down and we'll work it out. It's a misunderstanding! Ed—we'll work it out and we'll see Cora. We must see Cora. *We must see Cora, Ed!*

*Beat.* KATE *sits again.*

KATE: It's not complicated. We go over a few things. You allow yourself to… be known.

EDWARD: Known?

EMILY: Ed? Please, Ed!

KATE: And then you see Cora.

EDWARD *studies* KATE *for a few moments, taking in her terms.*

EDWARD: I am what you see.

*Beat.*

KATE: Edward Kingsley. An Ivy League MBA at twenty-three. A man certain of his destiny, comfortable in an Italian suit, perfectly pitched in the working arena between a responsible conservatism and a youthful openness to reform. Youngest Managing Director in the history of the company. Suddenly stranded.

*Pause.*

EDWARD: [*neutral, disconnected*] Stranded? [*Beat.*] Yes. Yes. That's fair.

KATE: A shock.

EDWARD: You see, I'm just awfully good at what I do.

KATE: What you *did*.

EDWARD: Whatever. Yes. Not a boast at all. There are things I'm—I have limited talents. My fashion sense is barbaric! I can't build a shed. But at certain things—Yes. Whatever we might be—here—in this house—we are not—distracted by the ordinariness of others. It's a vulgar thing to say—but in the privacy of my own house—I have never in my life been mediocre.

KATE: But the world *is*, isn't it?

*Beat. The fury begins.*

EDWARD: Some little, jumped-up nitwit in a double-breasted suit is using phrases like 'multi-skilling', brochures of new-model Saabs on his desk, and you're out the door, thank you very much! [*Beat.*] We sold the chalet—

EMILY: [*dryly*] Goodbye chalet…

EDWARD: We sold the boat.

EMILY: The boat vanishes…

EDWARD: I realised how much time we spent discussing things which were entirely dependent upon money. Of course, there is absolutely nothing more enjoyable to talk about, when one *has* money. When one doesn't, one leans towards other subjects: even the contemplation of—you might laugh—I would have laughed once—the contemplation of beauty. Yes. Beauty as a non-commodity.

KATE: You felt very let down, didn't you?

*Beat.*

EDWARD: [*losing strength, sadly*] Yes, I felt let down.

KATE: And your wife—she was sympathetic, but somehow that only made things worse, didn't it?

EMILY: Friendship, you see, doesn't get tested all that much in the nice suburbs. Those of us who live here—well, we are frightened of being discovered.

KATE: Discovered?

EMILY: The nights alone in our houses. Hiding. Crouched behind the Biedemeier dining suites. We don't think we'll be loved. So we don't invite help. We live here to blend. Yes. To blend. Sorrow singles us out—which is to be—to be feared—so we build solid walls around it— [*Beat.*] He held himself together. For me. For Cora.

KATE: But underneath, you were beginning to—

EDWARD: Well—

KATE: Unravel.

EDWARD: No! No I never—

KATE: Nothing anyone would notice. But moments. Private moments.

EDWARD *thinks about what she has said.*

EDWARD: It wasn't (easy)—

KATE: Thoughts that were not—safe. Ideas that came to you from somewhere… foreign.

EDWARD: The same friends I'd discuss things with—buying things—now carefully avoided showing me the brochures of the Bang and Olufsen CD player, the new Audi.

KATE: They pitied you.

EDWARD: [*the fury welling up*] *I hated their sensitivity!*—Their civility made me… It made me physically sick. There was a moment with Ken Whiting at the club when he put his arms around my shoulders and squeezed me. He squeezed me! 'Screw the bastards', he said. I had to excuse myself, ran down the corridor to the men's room to throw up, knocking over the trophy case on the way. Davis Steger offered me a loan! A loan! To me! There were times I wanted to—on the golf course… at the club… When I wanted to shut them up, just shut them up, to silence these *banalities*—when they had no idea—no idea—I just wanted to—I had to push it away—the vision of Ken Whiting and Ted Deakin drinking in the club lounge so full of goodwill—so *drunk* on goodwill—and me picking up the fire poker and bringing it down on them, bringing it down on them… smashing it down… smashing it… the blood…

*He breaks off, realising what he has said. Beat.*

KATE: And that's when it started—

*Beat.*

EMILY: When what—?

KATE: The business.

*Beat.*

EDWARD: [*still shaken*] What business?

*Beat.*

KATE: With Cora.

*Beat.*

EDWARD: What kind of—? *What* business?

KATE *is silent.*

EMILY: What? What is this?

EDWARD: What?

KATE: Those nights.

EDWARD: What?

KATE: I think you know.

EDWARD: What?!

*Silence.*

You think that I—? You think that I—? What are you—?

KATE: Let's stay calm—

EDWARD: What is it you're—? Just say what it is you're insinuating—? Where did this—?

EMILY: I don't understand. I just don't understand what's being said.

EDWARD: Cora never said—Cora never—No!

EMILY: Cora—what? What didn't Cora—?

EDWARD: Where did this all—? How could you invent something so— This is diabolical! This is just a diabolical—! This is an outrage!

KATE: You can argue with an opinion, Ed. But you cannot argue with a memory.

EDWARD: A memory?

KATE: Cora's memory.

EDWARD: [*astonished*] You say that Cora—that Cora—*remembered*—

KATE: A memory is not a matter of opinion.

EDWARD: Well, what if it is? *What if it is?* [*Pause. Quietly*] You think I have something to tell?

KATE: After nightfall.

EMILY: What is she talking about? What is she—?

EDWARD: I don't believe—?! You're telling me I—You're—That's sick! That's completely—! That's sick! You are sickening me! You are making me—

KATE: Now why does a sixteen-year-old girl, doing well in school, popular, seemingly well-balanced, suddenly run away from home and hide herself, hide herself *for seven years* without once contacting her parents? What was she running from? Who was she hiding from?

EDWARD: That's the whole point. We don't know.

*Beat.*

EMILY: For seven years. For seven years we have—Let me tell you, Ms Saskell—I'm not sure what you're saying here—I'm not sure I—But I can assure you that the last seven years have been—[*breaking*] have been—If you are a mother, if you are a mother, then surely, surely you understand what we have put ourselves through? The questions. The questions.

KATE: I think—you can answer those questions.

*Beat.*

EMILY: Me? You think I know?

KATE: Yes, Emily. I think you do know.

EMILY: [*urgently*] Ed?

EDWARD: Emily—listen—

EMILY: Ed?

EDWARD: I don't know what this is about—I don't know—

EMILY: Is she misunderstanding something, Ed?

EDWARD: I don't know—

EMILY: These days everything looks—everything looks—suspicious—

EDWARD: Emily—I don't—I don't—

EMILY: We all need to ask ourselves why. Why are we so in awe of innocence? Why do we disbelieve it so?

EDWARD: I have no idea—No idea—

EMILY: Did? Did something? Did something—? Ed—?

EDWARD: [*desperately*] Jesus, Emily!

EMILY: What is she—? I'm just asking you—Why is she here? Why is she punishing us? Why didn't Cora come? What is she talking about, Ed? I have to—I mean I have to—I have to *ask*—Ed—

EDWARD *shocked, holds his head in his hands.*

[*To* KATE] Cora said this? Cora said to you—?

KATE: You reap what you sew.

EMILY: You reap—? What? What is it that we have sewn?

EDWARD: It's mad. It's completely mad. You want me to say I—

KATE: You cannot deny. And Cora will not let you. Not any more. No. You see? She is no longer prepared to collude—

EDWARD: To collude—?

KATE: To perpetuate the silence. Because the silence will—kill her.

EMILY: What? What does she want you to—?

EDWARD: Emily—This woman is saying—this woman is saying that somehow, I—in those years—over that period—that I was 'dishevelled' enough—that I was perverted and sick enough to—

*Long silence as she absorbs the meaning.*

EMILY: But that's—? Look, Ms Saskell, look, I understand you're concerned for Cora. And believe me, anyone who has been concerned for Cora over these years is—is someone of great merit to us—Yes—But if this is coming from—if Cora suggested—if that is true and I find it hard—but if it is true, then something has happened to Cora. Something very bad has happened. Drugs.

KATE: Drugs?

EMILY: During those seven years—those years—something has twisted her—something evil has gotten hold of her—

KATE: Is that what you think?

EMILY: Well, what else?! My husband is not a—he is not a—He is not the kind of man—I've been married to him for twenty-nine years. I know my husband. He's the kindest and gentlest of—

KATE: Let's not fall into those—

EDWARD: Fall into—!

KATE: No—

EMILY: My husband is not a bad man. No, Ms Saskell. No. My husband has been a wonderful father. A wonderful, tender, loving, responsible father. The best father a girl—

KATE: Indeed—

EMILY: A girl could ask for. An exemplary father. I don't think I'm kidding myself—Superlative.

KATE: Superlative.

EMILY: And thoroughly normal.

KATE: Is 'normal' a defence. You tell me, is it good to be normal?

EMILY: [*confused*] Well—I mean—

KATE: It's in everyone's interest to perpetuate the myth of commonplace goodness.

EMILY: But we were—we *are* normal!

KATE: *This is normal.* What I'm talking about. Cora's history. Don't you realise that?

EMILY: [*agitated*] No. No, *I don't*. I know there are bad things—I know there are terrible things—well, probably right around the corner. But there are *good* things—there are very good—The Baillieaus, the—the Woolcotts—Terry and Frances up the—up the street—they started Neighbourhood Watch! Terry coaches Little League! The McIntyres! They put their son in de-tox—*He went to them*—The McIntyres are good people! We all are! We all are! They're everywhere! You cannot see the world so bleakly! What do you have left?

KATE: Truth.

EMILY: What do you have to believe in if you see the world that way?

KATE: You believe in righting it. You'd be surprised what goes on inside the walls of a suburban Spanish Mission. The things that happen within the pristine grounds of a Cape Cod-style white weatherboard. Evil sometimes comes covered in climbing roses.

EDWARD: Jesus!

EMILY: You think I know—?

EDWARD: Jesus! Emily! You can't go down that—How could you know something that did not, that could not happen?!

EMILY: You think that Ed, who loved—who loved—you think he could—?

KATE: 'This is *my* house and *my* child'. Do you listen to your husband?

EDWARD: Isn't there enough misery in the universe already? Without inventing it? Without tracking decent people down in their decent houses?

KATE: With their leather-bound classics. With their library ladders and their Waterford decanters?

EDWARD: *Yes, with their Waterford decanters!* You snob! You fucking snob! You're part of it, aren't you? This snide army of cynics invading our bureaucracies and our schools and our art; bankrupting us, brainwashing our children, intent on crushing innocence, determined to find hypocrisy lurking in the corners of houses full of books and rugs; taking your little torches into our psyches!

KATE: Books and rugs! Books and rugs!

EDWARD: You enter people's houses—you enter their sacred spaces and you search—you search—you get down on your knees and you look through bones and into dreams, into thoughts, flights of fancy, searching, searching for something, *anything* that might answer for your grief and your loss and your terror—

KATE: Your sacred spaces! Where you sit and nurture yourself with a vision of God. He's sitting there next to you in his corduroy pants and expensive woollen sweater mixing a gin and tonic and looking forward to settling in for the evening with the *Guardian Weekly*. And you love your God because your God loves you, you spineless little man. *Your God loves you*. And I can see you—yes, I can see you—because I have no God. *No God watches over me*. I've been wasted. I've been tossed out. And it has made me strong. Yes! It has made me strong.

EDWARD: [*quietly*] Or has it made you lonely? [*Beat.*] Tell me this, with your dark rooms and your embrace of catastrophe, do you stop? Do you ever stop? Do you sometimes, in a strange, unruly moment, ask yourself: What if? What if—When all is said and done—*What If I'm Wrong?*

*Silence.*

KATE: No.

*Pause.*

EMILY: [*lost in her own world*] You think I know?

KATE: [*to* EMILY] You loved him. But loving someone does not exclude seeing their frailties. And he had frailties, did he not?

EDWARD: This is just mumbo-jumbo! This is just psycho-babble bullshit!

EMILY: Yes. [*Beat.*] Yes, he had frailties.

EDWARD: Emily!

EMILY: Well, Ed? I mean, that's the truth, isn't it?

EDWARD: Jesus!

EMILY: You think I knew that Ed was—? You think that if something like that was happening and I knew, that I would not protect my child?

KATE: Your silence was wrong—but it was not contradictory with love.

*Silence.*

EMILY: And the only way that Cora will—the only way I can see Cora—?

*Silence.*

[*Dawning on her*] Ed? [*Beat.*] Ed? Listen, Ed—Listen, Ed—Just—Let's just—

EDWARD: No.

EMILY: Ed—Just—Think about it—If we—

EDWARD: No.

EMILY: [*desperately*] If it's the only—If it's the only—And then we can talk to Cora. Then we can talk and we can sort it all—Only, *we need to talk to Cora.*

EDWARD: Not if I—I—No, Emily—

EMILY: Just to see Cora. Listen, Ed. Listen, Ed. *I have to see Cora.*

EDWARD: And *I* don't? *And I don't?* And I don't have to see her?! What do you—? What do you think? That I don't feel the same—

EMILY: I know you do—I know you do—But this is the only way—This is the only way—And if you just—say—just make it up—just say—whatever—

KATE: No, Emily. No. It's not just words—

EMILY: [*ignoring* KATE] —And I won't even listen and you won't listen to me. It will just be in this vacuum. For her. For her. For Ms Saskell. And then she can go to Cora and say that we—we admitted—

EDWARD: No!

EMILY: [*desperately*] And then Cora will come. And we can see her!

Ed, we could see her! Cora. In front of us. Sitting there. There. In that chair. With her sweet face and her blue eyes and her strawberry-blonde—her—

EDWARD: Don't!

EMILY: [*softly, gently*] And then it wouldn't matter. It wouldn't matter because she would be here. And we could gently, gently, we could talk to her and I'm sure we could—With help. She could get over—She could—

EDWARD: [*quietly, astonished*] *You could say that?* [*Beat.*] You could say that you—? [*Beat. Soft, confiding, desperate*] Emily, I couldn't say the words.

*Beat.*

EMILY: Imagine this. Imagine this. A piece of paper. And on it is written three things: 'Cora', '2 a.m.' and 'secret'. Those three things. And just for today, just for this—purpose—you have to make up a story. Only not a story for children. A bad story. A horror story. And it has to be convincing. And you make it up and it's easy. It's easy because you and I know it isn't true. It's not true. It's just a game.

EDWARD: 'Cora'. '2 a.m.' 'Secret'.

EMILY: That's right.

EDWARD: Emily—No! No—I couldn't—I couldn't say the words.

EMILY: Listen. Listen to that sound. [*Beat.*] Listen to that word. [*Beat.*] It's over. It's over almost as soon as it's said.

EDWARD: No.

EMILY: Ed, look at me. Look at me! Somewhere in this city—somewhere here, *here*! Cora is waiting.

EDWARD: How could she—? How could—?

EMILY: We'll find out. And we'll fix it. But Ed, we can't go on anymore. I can't wait anymore for Cora. I'm telling you now, I'd rather be dead than hang on another day. And I know you—I know—(you feel the same.) [*Beat.*] Whatever it takes. Whatever. Let's just do it. Let's do it to see Cora.

EDWARD: [*angrily*] I'm not going to—And you can't! No, you can't! I won't let you—I won't—You cannot give in to this, Emily. Who is she? Who is she and what is she doing to us? You're going to let her walk into our house and say these things and *get away with it?* It's insane. It's insane and I won't let you.

EMILY: You won't let me?

EDWARD: I won't let you!

KATE: [*to* EMILY] This is what he does—Do you see? Do you see?

EMILY: He won't—

KATE: He sees it as his right. It's been twenty-nine years of forfeiting your own judgement, hasn't it Emily? Of doing what he bids you to do, of saying what he approves of, of forgetting what he requires you to forget—

EDWARD: That's not—! This is absurd—this went out with—You say you're a mother—Are you a mother?

KATE: How dare you—

EDWARD: To whom, Ms Saskell? One daughter you say you have. Could it be that you have flesh and blood—?

KATE: How dare you—

EDWARD: Or is it *our* flesh and blood that you mother? Whose daughter are we talking about? Is it our daughter?

EMILY: [*terrified*] Ed! No, Ed!

EDWARD: *Where did our little girl go? Tell me where you took her? Tell me what you've done to her.*

KATE: What *I've* done to her! What *I've* done to her! Oh, you're a good man, aren't you Ed? You're a fine man.

EDWARD: Yes, I think I am a good man! I'm not perfect. I'm a human being. I have certain flaws, but if goodness means compassion and responsibility and conscience, then, fuck it, yes! Yes. Yes *I fucking am a good man.*

KATE: You claim goodness.

EDWARD: Yes, I do!

KATE: You claim conscience—

EDWARD: Yes! Yes!

KATE: And do you claim fidelity?

*Silence as* EDWARD *and* EMILY *absorb the meaning.*

EDWARD: [*shocked, quietly*] What? [*Beat.*] Who are you to—? Who are you to stand in—?

EMILY: It was a mistake!

EDWARD: For a few weeks—I lost my—I just lost myself—I lost my judgement—

KATE: You lost yourself and your judgement—

EDWARD: What are you—? It was a long time ago! It was the only mistake I ever made in twenty-nine years of marriage. And it's between me and Emily and no one else. And she has—she has—forgiven—

KATE: Oh she has, has she?

EDWARD: Yes she has!

KATE: What power did she have to do anything else? Her world was the B-grade version of your world.

EDWARD: That's patronising! That's—

KATE: What could Emily do when you betrayed her?

EDWARD: Jesus… Jesus…

EMILY: [*desperately*] It only happened once. In twenty-nine years of marriage, that's not so bad. He was—He'd been through a bad—

KATE: And you hadn't?

EMILY: It wasn't the same for me. My life was not my work—it didn't abandon me—

KATE: Your life was your husband and your daughter and they *both* abandoned you.

EMILY*, shocked, takes this in.*

[*Quietly*] You are betrayed by him. Used by him and then you are his defence counsel. He's trained you well, hasn't he?

*Beat.*

EMILY: [*quietly*] I loved him.

EDWARD: Emily—

KATE: [*gently*] How many times did Ed lose his judgement, Emily? What was it that Cora remembered?

EMILY: I felt less than nothing. I felt less than nothing. I wanted to—I can tell you, I wanted to vanish—

EDWARD: [*walking to her*] Emily—Emily—

*She walks away from him.*

EMILY: [*quietly building*] Cora. Composed us. Her life was our compass. Yes. Ed's interests—his intellectual interests—well, I try to keep up of course, but my natural instinct is—I'm just not all that interested. We discovered that very early on and we made our peace with it. It was worth it to us to have the stability and the companionship. And the trade-off was that the part of us which was alight as individuals, would have to be—extinguished.

KATE: Extinguished?

EMILY: Before marriage—I had—I had a—this sounds—well, when I entered a room, I carried with me the possibility of ignition—Ed too. All of us. That's what makes us—We lost that. And so Cora was it for us. It was an *agreement*. And when Ed was—when he had the—this woman—I wondered if I could—if anything could be depended upon. It seemed as if the universe had entered some very subtle chaos. Nothing worked as it should. Chemicals were altering human taste buds. The sky—even the sky—even the sky was being corrupted. It was as if the world was collapsing but couldn't see itself—And only I, only I could see it. I wanted to kill him, but where would that have left Cora and me? It wasn't the sex—It was the *intimacy*. That this woman would get that precious intimacy, which is more sexual than sex, the light-heartedness, the flightiness, the enchantment which belongs only to illegitimate love and never to legitimate—I had earned it! I had earned it!

EDWARD: [*quietly*] Emily—

EMILY: No! No!

EDWARD: [*softly*] Don't you see, Emily, what she's doing? She's trying to divide us. We have to hold on together—we have to—You forgave me, Emily. Remember? Remember?

EMILY: [*distraught*] What choice did I have, Ed?

*She is silent.* EDWARD *is bewildered, shocked.*

That's why—Cora leaving gave us—It joined us—because only we—only we—understood what it was to be left. To be left. To be abandoned. The secrecy, the privacy, the aloneness of knowing that… cemented us. But is it love? Don't we call whatever it is that binds us 'love'? All of us? All of us—in these—in these *couples*. We call that love, because we cannot bear to name it! The companionship of despair. And now—perhaps this—We need to be shaken up! We need to be thrilled by disaster! Yes! Yes! We need to have our own sacred covenants trampled upon. Ed? Ed? How do we recognise love if we cannot recognise its absence? [*A long silence. And then she resolves*] Certain nights when we didn't go out. Cold nights.

EDWARD: Emily?

KATE: Go on—

EMILY: Often I just—I was sleeping—

KATE: Yes—That's good—

EMILY: I was sleeping. But sometimes. Every once in a—I'd wake and he wouldn't be there. And in the morning I'd say—

EDWARD: Emily?

EMILY: 'Last night'? And he'd—he'd—Say he couldn't sleep—He couldn't—He'd lost the job—had a lot on his—

EDWARD *takes her arm and pulls her aside.*

EDWARD: [*quietly, urgently frantic*] Let me say this to you. Let me say to you this. You cannot come back from the place you are going. There is no return. If you take this—if you go this—if you give them what they want, just be aware, we cannot get back to what we were, what we are. That will—vanish.

EMILY: [*hard*] *I have to see Cora.*

EDWARD: What is Cora? Tell me that? What is Cora now? What has she become?

EMILY: [*frantically*] I don't care. I don't care anymore. I don't care what else vanishes. I don't care what she has become. *I have to see my daughter again.* And if you don't think this is worth it—

EDWARD: [*urgently, desperate*] No! No! Because the truth is all we have, now!

EMILY: [*desperately*] Then you're a fool, Ed! I have to see her!

*She starts hitting him, weeping. He stands there, unmoving as she beats at him with her fists. She stops slowly, is left standing there, reduced to stillness. From this point on, it is impossible to know if she is inventing or remembering.*

[*Trance-like*] I used to see the house as—tilted—as tilted—as if it were losing confidence in gravity—

EDWARD: Emily? Emily, what are you—?

EMILY: I'm her mother. I didn't know. I didn't want to—But if I'm honest I'd have to say that there was something different—at that time—Something I couldn't quite—

EDWARD: Listen to me! Listen to me! Emily! You can't give in to this—

EMILY: It wasn't easy to see—It wasn't easy to—She was eleven years old but she had lost her—girlishness—there was a sweetness missing—the light had gone out of her—There was a spark missing.

EDWARD: [*disbelieving*] A spark missing?

EMILY: As if there were a layer of glass between her physical form and the rest of her existence. She started to float—

EDWARD: To float—

EMILY: Ed said: She's growing up. She's. Look at her. She's almost a young woman now.

EDWARD: [*genuinely confused*] And that's—what?—suspicious? Is that—tell me, because perhaps I'm living in a completely outdated world, but is that wrong for a father to say—?

EMILY: Not wrong. No. Accurate. And I let it go at that. Because I did not want to be faced with a situation in which I had a duty that I could not… fulfill. A duty to say. To speak.

EDWARD: Emily? Do you—? Are you—? Is this for them? Is this for them or are you really—?

EMILY: She's right, Ed. I want to say it.

EDWARD: [*panicked*] But is this for them, Emily? Just tell me. Just tell me!

EMILY: I want to say it. I want it to be spoken.

EDWARD: [*quiet, shocked*] Spoken?

EMILY: This could be—Look, Ed—we haven't——We haven't had—This might be good for us. Both of us silently allowing… allowing standards of personal—dignity—to fade—to fade—This way—perhaps—some atonement—some—is that too grand?—Some atonement?

EDWARD: [*so sad, so shocked*] All we have lived through. All we have faced together.

EMILY: It won't be over, Ed. It won't all be (over)—Once it's said out loud, we can start again. And Cora will be with us.

EDWARD: What? My God, Emily! What are you saying? I did not do anything. I DID NOT DO ANYTHING!

EMILY: [*trance-like*] I had woken and the bed was empty. I walked out of the bedroom and down the hall to Cora's room. I stood outside the door, the air in the room, the sounds of—of—the sounds of— [*Beat.*] Is that passion? Perhaps—perhaps—passion is *always* somehow—corrupt—perhaps passion *has to* transgress something—

*Beat.*

EDWARD: [*deeply shocked*] You heard that?

*Silence.* EMILY *does not look at him.*

Emily—look at me. Look at me and tell me that you heard that.

*She refuses to look.*

Tell me, Emily! Tell me that you heard that! Have I—? Am I—? [*Beat.*] How could you say the words?

*Silence.*

[*Sadly, quietly*] Our little girl.

*Silence.*

EMILY: [*quietly, almost to herself*] What have I done?

EDWARD: The night she was born, she was so angry!… Yes… Yes, perhaps—Perhaps—

EMILY: [*dawning on her*] What have I done? Ed? Ed? WHAT HAVE I DONE?!

EDWARD: [*as if it's coming to him*] Perhaps—yes. *Yes*. I can—I can feel it now—Yes… That's right… Those nights. Yes… And it never felt—it never felt—with nightfall comes—its own country. The darkness has its own character, doesn't it?

EMILY: Ed?

EDWARD: Yes—Cora is such a beauty—Yes, yes that's right—And it wasn't possible—it simply wasn't possible to resist… to resist the chance of—*owning*—her… I loved—perhaps—yes. Too much. Nightfall. Yes. Emily asleep. Yes.

EMILY: Ed?

EDWARD: A dream overtaking me—

EMILY: Ed? No! No!

EDWARD: [*ignoring her*] And Cora silent—Yes!—Yes!—

EMILY: No—No, Ed! No—I've changed my—*Don't*, Ed—Please, Ed—don't—

EDWARD: She simply chose to stay silent—

EMILY: Ed? Ed? Are you—? Is this—?

EDWARD: And if something is never said—it begins to—it starts to appear to you—as a 'figment'—as something one might have imagined once. Yes. [*Beat.*] Yes. [*Beat.*] And now—?

*The three of them sit quite still.* KATE *gets up and walks to the window and looks out. She makes a small motion with her hand. As she walks back and gathers her bag and her coat all three turn their heads towards the front door. The doorbell rings.*

*Blackout.*

THE END